everyday
courage

everyday courage

---

365 WAYS TO A FEARLESS LIFE

CONTRIBUTING EDITOR: EMMA HILL

FIREFLY BOOKS

A FIREFLY BOOK

Published by Firefly Books Ltd. 2017

First printing

Publisher Cataloging-in-Publication Data (U.S.)

Library of Congress Cataloging-in-Publication Data is available

Library and Archives Canada Cataloguing in Publication

    Everyday courage : 365 ways to a fearless life / contributing editor, Emma Hill.
ISBN 978-1-77085-993-7 (softcover)

    1. Courage--Quotations, maxims, etc. 2. Courage--Miscellanea. 3. Self-actualization (Psychology). 4. Affirmations.
I. Hill, Emma, (Emma Elizabeth), editor
BF575.C8E94 2017   158   C2017-901729-2

Published in the United States by
Firefly Books (U.S.) Inc.
P.O. Box 1338, Ellicott Station
Buffalo, New York 14205

Published in Canada by
Firefly Books Ltd.
50 Staples Avenue, Unit 1
Richmond Hill, Ontario L4B 0A7

Printed in China

First published by Bounty Books,
a division of Octopus Publishing Group Ltd
Carmelite House
50 Victoria Embankment
London, EC4Y 0DZ

For Bounty Books
Publisher: Lucy Pessell; Designer: Lisa Layron; Design: Ummagumma; Contributing editor: Emma Hill; Editor: Sarah Vaughan; Production manager: Caroline Alberti; Images: Shutterstock/Irtsya

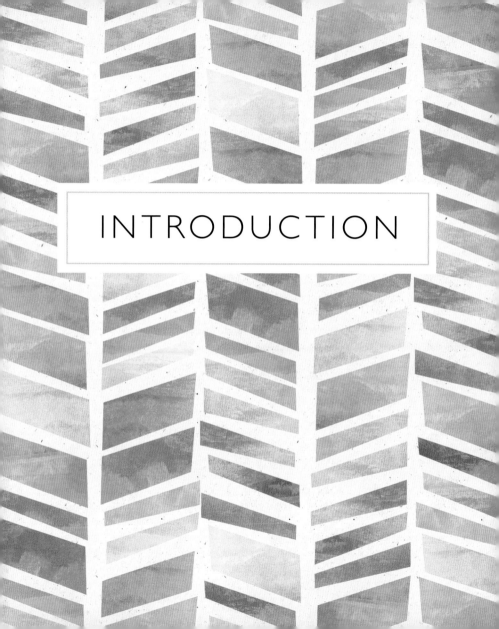

INTRODUCTION

Courage (noun):

the ability to do something that frightens one; bravery.

"She called on all her courage to face the ordeal."

Being courageous is not about having no fear. Quite the opposite. It's about being fearful, but going ahead anyway. It's about having the confidence to embrace change, forge relationships, aim for new horizons and reach for the stars. Courage is about facing your fears head-on, embodying a positive mindset, accepting your vulnerabilities, learning from mistakes, picking yourself up and carrying on. Being fearless is not about embarking on adrenaline junkie activities such as jumping out of a plane or launching yourself from a bridge attached to a bungee cord. While such adventures can ignite the spirit, they have very little to do with real bravery. True courage is about conquering the intangible fears we face on a daily basis. And the best news? Courage can be learned.

When we work on developing our courage, we empower ourselves with the ability to confront problems head-on, as well as acquiring the skills needed to grow and live a full life. *Everyday Courage* will be an invaluable companion in this quest for fearless living, providing an exercise, tip or inspirational quote for every day of the year to help boost your bravery. Some of these pages focus on building your self-confidence, an essential component in cultivating courage; others provide advice and ideas on how you can overcome your fears, find perspective and embrace life's challenges.

Don't let another year slip through your fingers in the blink of an eye. Use this book as your guide, inspiration and motivation to embrace a year of courageous living.

MAKE A START

Whatever it is you want to do, whatever fears are holding you back, whatever excuses you've been giving yourself, do one thing today that takes a step toward your goal.
Stop procrastinating and begin.

"Every adventure requires a first step."

– THE CHESHIRE CAT,
ALICE IN WONDERLAND

"He who is not everyday
conquering some fear
has not learned the
secret of life."

– RALPH WALDO EMERSON

DISTANCE YOURSELF FROM YOUR THOUGHTS

If you are having a thought that undermines your attempt at bravery, simply notice it and tell yourself "oh there's a fearful thought." By paying attention to your thoughts and labeling them in this non-judgmental, conscious way you are distancing yourself from the thought itself and as such are far less likely to let it influence your behavior.

"She stood in the storm,
and when the wind did
not blow her away,
she adjusted her sails."

– ELIZABETH EDWARDS

LISTEN TO YOUR HEART

Not just a clichéd line from many a ballad, listening to that inner voice takes courage. If you can tune into this it will give you the greatest insight into where you want to be heading and what you need to do in order to get there.

"Anything's possible if you've got enough nerve."

– J.K. ROWLING

NAME YOUR FEAR

Sometimes we can't quite pin down what it is that we're scared of and this uncertainty only increases anxiety. Find some time to sit in silence and engage in self-reflection to identify exactly what it is you're afraid of.

"You cannot swim for new horizons until you have courage to lose sight of the shore."

– WILLIAM FAULKNER

SAY YES

If your inner voice is screaming out for you to agree to
something, but your fear of the unknown is holding you back
and repeatedly leads to you turning down opportunities —
whether it be a drink with a colleague you don't know that
well, a new job opportunity or a transformational haircut —
then it's time to start saying "yes" more often!

"Believe you can and you're halfway there."

– THEODORE ROOSEVELT

"You can make whatever you want out of your life, but first you have to not be afraid to try."

– UNKNOWN

TAKE SMALL STEPS

One way to face fear head-on is by taking small steps. Anything seems more achievable once broken down into bite-sized pieces. Tackling things one step at a time takes your focus away from the bigger, scarier picture. Before you know it you will be well on your way to achieving your goal without having broken a sweat!

"The hardest step
she ever took was
to blindly trust in
who she was."

– ATTICUS

"Bran thought about it.
'Can a man still be brave
if he's afraid?'
'That is the only time a
man can be brave,'
his father told him."

– GEORGE R.R. MARTIN,
A GAME OF THRONES

FILL YOUR MIND WITH COURAGE

If fear is holding you back from making that first move toward accomplishing a goal, fill your mind with courageous thoughts: think about others in a similar situation to yourself who have made the move; read real-life stories of bravery; study figures in history who have shown great courage. Let them be your inspiration and your motivation.

"The most courageous act is still to think for yourself. Aloud."

– COCO CHANEL

DO IT FOR YOU

Set goals and challenges that are meaningful to you.
Don't worry about what anyone else thinks about them —
you don't need anybody's approval — do them just for you.

"I learned that courage was not the absence of fear, but the triumph over it. The brave man is not he who does not feel afraid, but he who conquers that fear."

– NELSON MANDELA

"Courage is grace under pressure."

– ERNEST HEMINGWAY

DON'T BE AFRAID OF FAILURE

If you are too afraid to make a mistake then you will never step out into the arena. Acknowledge the fact that making mistakes is just a part of the human condition and make peace with this. Each mistake will bring newfound knowledge, valuable lessons and insights. Learn from them and then move on.

"Don't be afraid of your fears. They're not there to scare you. They're there to let you know that something is worth it."

– C. JOYBELL C.

"Success is not final,
failure is not fatal:
it is the courage
to continue that
counts."

— SIR WINSTON CHURCHILL

REWARD YOURSELF

Don't let your achievements go unnoticed. Every time you make a courageous decision or face your fears, however big or small, reward yourself. Give yourself a virtual pat on the back, whether it's treating yourself to a night out, a day off or a large slice of cake.

"Just because you fail once doesn't mean you're gonna fail at everything."

– MARILYN MONROE

DON'T BE AFRAID OF FEAR

If the thing you fear is fear itself you will never find the motivation to pursue your dreams. Instead, you will get stuck in a self-perpetuating cycle of inaction. Often we want fear to go away before we take action. However, that's not how it works — fear doesn't just disappear. You have to swat it away or plow through it, circle around it…In other words you move ahead in spite of it.

"What would life
be if we had
no courage to
attempt anything?"

– VINCENT VAN GOGH

"What if I fall?
Oh, but my darling,
what if you fly?"

- ERIN HANSON

"You gain strength, courage, and confidence by every experience in which you really stop to look fear in the face. Do the thing you think you cannot do."

– ELEANOR ROOSEVELT

MAKE A LIST

Write a list of all the things you would do right now if fear weren't holding you back. Perhaps it's requesting a pay raise, leaving a relationship, changing career, moving city, starting a new class, asking someone on a date…List these in order of least fearful to most fearful. Start at the top and work your way down. As you begin to check off the easiest targets on your list, so your confidence and courage will grow and enable you to tackle the really scary stuff.

"You get in life what you have the courage to ask for."

– OPRAH WINFREY

TAKE COLD SHOWERS

While it may not sound like the bravest act in the world, this is a really simple way to cultivate courage on a daily basis. Your mind will resist stepping into the shower, but you can face the fear (or at least reticence) and overcome this resistance each and every morning, and probably learn in the process that it's not as bad as your mind led you to believe it would be.

"Until you step into the unknown, you don't know what you're made of."

– ROY T. BENNETT

"Courage isn't having the strength to go on — it is going on when you don't have strength."

– NAPOLEON BONAPARTE

DWELL ON YOUR PAST ACHIEVEMENTS

Bring to mind all the times in your life when you have acted courageously, when you faced your fears and took a leap into the unknown with successful outcomes. Close your eyes and focus on how that made you feel. Let these feelings inspire you to once again act with bravery.

"Courage is doing what you are afraid to do. There can be no courage unless you are scared."

– EDDIE RICKENBACKER

"I have accepted fear as part of life — specifically the fear of change…I have gone ahead despite the pounding in the heart that says: turn back…"

– ERICA JONG

STEP OUT OF YOUR COMFORT ZONE

Psychological research increasingly suggests that growth occurs at the edge of our comfort zone. So get uncomfortable. You don't necessarily have to parachute out of a plane to leave your comfort territory; you could try a new food, enroll in an evening class, dance in public, travel somewhere you've never been before, listen to a different genre of music…

"You never change your
life until you step out
of your comfort zone;
change begins at the end
of your comfort zone."

– ROY T. BENNETT

"I believe that the most
important single thing,
beyond discipline and
creativity is daring to dare."

– MAYA ANGELOU

"Fall seven times,
stand up eight."

– STEPHEN BUSH

CHOOSE YOUR FRIENDS WISELY

Surround yourself with positive people who believe in you.
Developing courage requires a certain level of self-esteem, so be
friends only with people who boost your confidence and urge
you to follow your dreams.

FEBRUARY 12TH

"You are braver than you believe, stronger than you seem, and smarter than you think."

– CHRISTOPHER ROBIN, *WINNIE THE POOH*

"Life shrinks or
expands in proportion
to one's courage."

– ANAÏS NIN

USE HUMOROUS IMAGERY

Take the power away from your fear by imagining it
as a funny little creature. Give it whatever amusing features
your imagination conjures up. Then finally give it wings and
watch it fly away.

"Freedom lies in being bold."

– ROBERT FROST

"Use your fear…
it can take you to
the place where you
store your courage."

– AMELIA EARHART

DAILY COURAGE

Challenge yourself to do one small thing each day to push your boundaries and increase your fear threshold. This could be anything from going to the movies by yourself, sparking up a conversation with someone who you admire, asking a friend for a favor…whatever it may be that makes you feel uncomfortable. This is a way of maintaining a courageous mindset, without having to necessarily make panic-inducing, life-changing decisions on a daily basis.

"Every great dream begins with a dreamer. Always remember, you have within you the strength, the patience, and the passion to reach for the stars to change the world."

– HARRIET TUBMAN

FOCUS ON
THE POSITIVE

When trying to motivate yourself to take the first step in accomplishing a goal envisage positive outcomes. Focus on how great you would feel, and how improved your life would be instead of getting caught up in thoughts of what might go wrong.

"She was unstoppable.
Not because she did not have
failures or doubts, but because
she continued on despite them."

– BEAU TAPLIN

DITCH PERFECTIONISM

The quest for perfection is so often what stops us in our tracks before we've even begun. We're afraid that we can't do something perfectly and so we don't even try. Studies have shown that perfectionists actually tend to be less successful people than those who accept setbacks and learn from them. So today let go of the desire to be perfect and do everything perfectly — it will only ever impede your progress.

"Failure is unimportant.
It takes courage to make
a fool of yourself."

– CHARLIE CHAPLIN

BLOW YOUR OWN TRUMPET

Cultivate self-confidence by completing the following sentences:

I love my…

My friends would tell you I'm…

I am great at…

My best quality is…

I feel good about…

"If you feel like quitting think about why you started."

– UNKNOWN

"A ship is safe
in harbor, but
that's not what
ships are for."

– WILLIAM G.T. SHEDD

ACCEPT YOUR LIMITATIONS

Nobody can do all things all of the time. If, for example, you're trying to find the courage to embark on a new exercise regime, accept that you will not immediately be able to run 10k. It's fine to start off walking. With everything that you are trying to achieve, it's fine to begin slowly. Beginning at all is what's important.

"Be brave, take risks. Nothing can substitute experience."

– PAULO COELHO

"With courage you will dare to take risks, have the strength to be compassionate, and the wisdom to be humble. Courage is the foundation of integrity."

– MARK TWAIN

MAKE YOUR OWN MANTRAS

Mantras are positive affirmations that help to cultivate a more optimistic mindset. Make your own and repeat them each morning before you start your day. Some ideas to get you started:

- I believe in myself.

- I know that I can accomplish anything I set my mind on.

- I have the courage to step into my future with grace and ease.

- I am worthy of achieving everything I wish for.

"You've always had
the power, my dear,
you just had to learn
it for yourself."

– GLINDA,
THE WONDERFUL WIZARD OF OZ

"Bravery is the
solution to regret."

– ROBIN SHARMA

FIND A MENTOR

Look amongst the people you know for anyone who has faced adversity in a courageous manner. Ask them how they made their decisions, overcame their fears and confronted their obstacles. Take as much advice as you can from the bravest person in your life.

"Courage is what it takes to stand up and speak. Courage is also what it takes to sit down and listen."

– SIR WINSTON CHURCHILL

PLAN FOR ANY OBSTACLES YOU MIGHT FACE

When it comes to chasing dreams, be realistic and recognize that you will most likely face obstacles along the way. Acknowledging this and planning for any setbacks means that when they happen they won't knock you off course. You can just calmly put your plans for overcoming them into action.

ADMIT THAT YOU'RE SCARED

Courage isn't the absence of fear. It's going ahead in spite of the fear. So acknowledge that you're scared, either by verbalizing it or writing it down. When you are this honest about your emotions, they are much easier to deal with.

"You have to accept whatever comes and the only important thing is that you meet it with courage and with the best that you have to give."

– ELEANOR ROOSEVELT

"Be somebody nobody thought you could be."

– UNKNOWN

DON'T FOCUS ON YOUR FLAWS

Focusing on your flaws just taps into the mindset of fear and undermines your feelings of self-worth. There are always going to be some areas in which you're weaker than others but if you concentrate on these instead of your positive attributes you will end up feeling ashamed of yourself — an emotion not conducive to courageous actions.

"At any given moment you have the power to say:

This is not how the story is going to end."

– UNKNOWN

"Take the risk
or lose
the chance."

– UNKNOWN

ASK FOR HELP

You cannot do everything alone. Courage is not plowing
on unaided. It's braver to recognize your own vulnerabilities,
to acknowledge when you need help and to seek it, let it happen
and then give thanks for it.

"You can't get to courage without walking through vulnerability."

– BRENÉ BROWN

"You never know how strong you are until being strong is the only choice you have."

– BOB MARLEY

DON'T COMPARE YOURSELF TO OTHERS

Comparing yourself to where others are and what they might be achieving is a shortcut to damaging your self-confidence. Everyone has their own journey, with their own unique set of challenges. Focus on your own.

"Your only limit
is you."

– UNKNOWN

PRACTICE MINDFULNESS

Engage in mindfulness meditation to help you deal with negative thought patterns that may be holding you back. Try an app like Headspace and take just ten minutes out of each day for quiet contemplation.

"Fear is only
as deep as the
mind allows."

– JAPANESE PROVERB

"To overcome fear is the quickest way to gain your self-confidence."

– ROY T. BENNETT

IF IN DOUBT, FAKE IT

Psychological research has shown that "putting on a brave face,"
even when you're feeling far from brave, can actually help you
become braver. Act as if you have no fear and the chances are
you will naturally become less fearful.

"Courage is being scared to death, but saddling up anyway."

– JOHN WAYNE

TAKE DEEP BREATHS

Simply breathe in slowly and deeply through your nose. Draw in the air and feel it fill your lungs. Now exhale slowly through your mouth. This will have an immediate calming effect, both physiologically — deep breathing triggers our parasympathetic nervous system which controls our fight or flight response — and psychologically. Do this throughout the day, whenever you need to quell your nerves to face your fears.

"It's better to be a lion for a day than a sheep all your life."

– SISTER ELIZABETH KENNY

USE YOUR EMOTIONS

Learning to harness your emotions is a huge step in cultivating courage. When focused, emotions can be used to spur you into action. Anger, for example, leaves no room for fear and can really help to boost your bravery. There is a fine balance to be struck here — too much anger can cloud your thoughts and judgments; just enough and it can become a valuable tool.

"Courage is the most important of all the virtues because without courage, you can't practice any other virtue consistently."

– MAYA ANGELOU

TRY THE
20-SECOND RULE

This idea stems from a line in the movie *We Bought a Zoo*. Matt Damon, who plays the role of Benjamin Mee, tells his son, "Sometimes all you need is 20 seconds of insane courage, just literally 20 seconds of embarrassing bravery, and I promise you something great will come of it." Whenever you need that extra boost of confidence, just remind yourself that you can do anything for 20 seconds!

"Be fearless in pursuit of what sets your soul on fire."

– UNKNOWN

"Man cannot discover
new oceans unless he
has the courage to lose
sight of the shore."

– ANDRÉ GIDE

WRITE YOUR OWN STORY

Literally. Put pen to paper and write what you would like to happen in your life right now. Doing this can help to consolidate your ambitions and hopes, as well as motivate you to make the story come true.

"All our dreams can come true, if we have the courage to pursue them."

– WALT DISNEY

IDENTIFY YOUR STRENGTHS

Self-confidence is an absolutely essential tool in cultivating courage. Boost your own by making a list of all of your strengths, your best character traits and values. Reminding yourself of all your positive attributes also makes them more likely to fire up when you need them.

"You are fierce.
You're a survivor.

You're a fighter through
and through.

Little brave, breathe.

There is a warrior
within you."

– BEAU TAPLIN

"Above all be the heroine of your life, not the victim."

– NORA EPHRON

GO SOMEWHERE YOU'VE NEVER BEEN BEFORE

Go on holiday to somewhere you've always wanted to go, take some time out to travel, go to that restaurant in town you've always liked the look of or simply walk a different way home. Dare to spice up your life with a little dose of variety.

"Sometimes the smallest step in the right direction ends up being the biggest step of your life. Tiptoe if you must, but take the step."

– UNKNOWN

"If it scares you,
it might be a good
thing to try."

– SETH GODIN

"Fear is a reaction.
Courage is a
decision."

– SIR WINSTON CHURCHILL

BUILD YOUR CONFIDENCE THROUGH SELF-AFFIRMATIONS

Repeat these self-affirmations throughout the day —
at any point when your confidence levels need a boost

- I accept myself for who I am.

- I am worthy of love.

- I deserve success.

"The greatest risk any of us will take is to be seen as we truly are."

– CINDERELLA

STAND UP FOR YOURSELF

Trust in yourself and your own instincts. Don't shy away from defending your actions. Have conviction in your opinions and behavior and don't let anybody talk you into or out of situations.

"It takes nothing to join the crowd. It takes everything to stand alone."

– HANS F. HANSEN

"Scared is what you're feeling. Brave is what you're doing."

– EMMA DONOGHUE, *ROOM*

"Replace fear
of the unknown
with curiosity."

– PENELOPE WARD

BE A BEGINNER

As children we were unafraid to climb the tallest tree or fling ourselves down treacherous slopes in a toboggan, yet once we reach adulthood life has taught us to be fearful of many things. The sensible "what if" part of our brain kicks in and inhibits us in ways that we just weren't as children. Our knowledge of everything that could go wrong holds us back. Try to embrace the Zen Buddhism concept of "a beginner's mind" by ing the enthusiastic, curious, open mind of a child. Question what you would do if you weren't afraid.

"The one who falls and gets up is so much stronger than the one who never fell."

– UNKNOWN

"Be smart enough
to hold on.
Be brave enough
to let go."

– UNKNOWN

TAKE A BREAK FROM THE OLD ROUTINE

Gradually strengthen your ability to be courageous by stepping out of your comfort zone in small ways every day. Change up your routine — walk to work instead of driving, get up earlier, take a different route home, go out for dinner alone…anything that goes slightly against the grain for you will force you into different situations. You will find yourself making braver and bolder choices, however minor, instead of running on autopilot.

"Be brave enough
to travel the
unknown path,
and learn what you
are capable of."

– RACHEL WOLCHIN

EXPRESS YOURSELF

Don't feel that you have to conform to your peer group. Wear what makes you feel good regardless of whether or not it's in fashion or in keeping, listen to the music you like, watch the movies you love, read the books that inspire you…It's only when you are true to yourself in this way that you become comfortable in your own skin and so can live a full and courageous life.

"The greatest act of courage is to be and own all that you are. Without apology. Without excuses and without any masks to cover the truth of who you truly are."

– SANDI AMORIM

"Always do
what you are
afraid to do."

– RALPH WALDO EMERSON

DON'T OVER-ANALYZE

Whereas a certain amount of critical thinking is essential in our decision-making processes, it's all too easy to over-think situations when we're feeling less than brave about them. However, once we start over-analyzing, self-doubt creeps in, we come up with an array of hypothetical negative outcomes and we lose our confidence to go ahead. If your intuition is telling you to go for it, take action before the fear sets in. If it doesn't work out then chalk it up as experience and embrace the lessons learned for next time.

"Sometimes your only available transportation is a leap of faith."

– MARGARET SHEPARD

"Have the courage to follow your heart and intuition. They somehow know what you truly want to become."

– STEVE JOBS

MAKE YOUR VOICE BE HEARD

This has nothing to do with cranking up your vocal volume and everything to do with being opinionated. If you're not naturally this way inclined then read up on things and start making decisions about what matters to you, what your convictions are. Practice voicing these on a daily basis in a polite, clear and confident manner. Getting your voice heard is an essential component in building up self-confidence and therefore courage.

"Speak your mind, even if your voice shakes."

– MAGGIE SMITH

"It takes courage to grow up and become who you truly are."

– E.E. CUMMINGS

TALK TO SOMEONE YOU DON'T KNOW

Sparking up small talk with a stranger is a daunting thought to all but the most confident among us, but this is a great way to cultivate courage. So next time you're at a party or in a similar social situation, seek out someone you don't know to chat with.

"Courage is like a muscle; it is strengthened by use."

– RUTH GORDON

"In a gentle way,
you can shake
the world."

– MAHATMA GANDHI

JOURNAL YOUR BRAVERY

Try to develop awareness each time you do something you're scared of. You may well embark on courageous acts every day of your life without really noticing. This is particularly true if you're shy. Maybe you've had to stand up and give a presentation, speak out in a meeting, ask a stranger for directions…Start a journal and each night write down something you did that day that made you feel uncomfortable. Acknowledging these acts of courage, however small, will boost your confidence and encourage you to keep being brave.

"Stay afraid, but do it anyway.
What's important is the action.
You don't have to wait to be
confident. Just do it and eventually
the confidence will follow."

— CARRIE FISHER

"I've been absolutely terrified every moment of my life — and I've never let it keep me from doing a single thing I wanted to do."

– GEORGIA O'KEEFFE

"Courage is resistance to fear,
mastery of fear,
not absence of fear."

– MARK TWAIN

FIND COURAGE
IN NUMBERS

If embarking on a project solo seems too overwhelming, seek support from friends, family or colleagues. There is often safety in numbers — doing something as a group could provide just the impetus you need to get up and running.

"What good are wings without the courage to fly?"

– ATTICUS

USE VISUALIZATION

Visualize your fears as clouds floating across the sky.
Label each "worry cloud" as it floats past without passing
judgment. This is a really useful exercise in distancing yourself
from your fears. It helps you to recognize them as something
separate from yourself. Acknowledge the fact that they are
removed from you, not a part of your being and as such they do
not have to dictate your life.

"One of the bravest decisions you'll ever make is to finally let go of what is hurting your heart and soul."

– BRIGITTE NICOLE

"The greatest danger for most of us is not that our aim is too high and we miss it but that it is too low and we reach it."

– MICHELANGELO

FACE YOUR FEARS

Exposing yourself to your fears can be a really effective way of overcoming them. Look at how phobias are treated — if, for example, someone is afraid of snakes they are exposed to pictures and then the real thing, and next move on to handling the snake. Most people report a significant reduction in fear after going through this process. Think how you can apply this training to areas of your life, to your own personal fears. Shying away from them can really restrict your life and your potential for success and happiness.

"Everything you want is
on the other side
of fear."

– JACK CANFIELD

"Be brave.

Without bravery, you will never know the world as richly as it longs to be known.

Without bravery, your life will remain small — far smaller than you probably wanted your life to be."

– ELIZABETH GILBERT

"If we wait until we're ready, we'll be waiting for the rest of our lives."

– LEMONY SNICKET

"If you want something
you've never had,

you have to do something
you've never done."

– UNKNOWN

KEEP LEARNING

Enroll in evening classes, study, go on a course, research subjects you're interested in. Learn from people around you, ask questions, take every opportunity to hone a new skill, read books…The more knowledge you have the less risks you have to take in order to be successful in your quests.

"You'll never do a whole lot unless you're brave enough to try."

– DOLLY PARTON

STAND UP FOR OTHERS

If you're in a situation where people are gossiping unkindly about somebody, or someone in a vulnerable position is being talked down to, speak out for them. Feel your confidence grow as you become the voice for someone who is being treated unfairly.

"Having a soft heart
in a cruel world is
courage,
not weakness."

– UNKNOWN

"The biggest mistake you could ever make is being too afraid to make one."

– UNKNOWN

SET A SMALL GOAL...
AND ACHIEVE IT

Set yourself a very attainable goal. Once you have accomplished this, tick it off your list and set to work on a new goal. Keep going in this way, setting and achieving small goals. It's a great way to build up your confidence, setting you up to tackle ever more courageous tasks.

"If you are lucky enough to find a way of life you love, you have to find the courage to live it."

– JOHN IRVING

"You can, you should, and if you're brave enough to start, you will."

– STEPHEN KING

CHOOSE WHICH OF YOUR ABILITIES TO DEVELOP

Being good at things is a great way to build self-confidence, so take some time out to analyze your abilities. Identify what you're good at, what will be of most use to you in the future and make the decision to work more on those skills. Don't fall into the trap of thinking you have to be good at everything. This is impossible. Simply choose which of your skills to develop and hone to give you the best chance at becoming a self-confident, courageous individual.

"You don't have to see the whole staircase, just take the first step."

– MARTIN LUTHER KING

START SOMETHING NEW

If you have a love of cooking, take up cookery lessons. If you have artistic tendencies, enroll in a painting course…whatever you have a passion for that you haven't yet indulged in. It takes courage to start something new, to go back to being a beginner in a room of experts. This is a great way to build up your sense of self-worth.

"If somebody offers you an amazing opportunity but you are not sure you can do it, say yes — then learn how to do it later!

– RICHARD BRANSON

"If you could get up the courage to begin, you have the courage to succeed."

– DAVID VISCOTT

"Don't shrink your dreams. Super-size your courage and abilities."

– KAREN SALMANSOHN

THINK POSITIVE

Negativity inhibits us in so many ways, holding us back from accomplishing our goals, damaging our self-confidence and feelings of self-worth. Today, every time a negative thought comes into your head, replace it with a positive one. This is much easier than it sounds and you'll be amazed at the results!

"Always believe in yourself. Do this and no matter where you are you will have nothing to fear."

– HAYAO MIYAZAKI

"Courage is a love affair with the unknown."

– OSHO

"I am always doing things I can't do; that's how I get to do them."

– PABLO PICASSO

"A strong woman looks a challenge dead in the eye and gives it a wink."

– GINA CAREY

DO IT TO BECOME COURAGEOUS

We become courageous by doing the things we fear. So we can't wait to feel brave before we take action. We take action in spite of the fear and as a consequence become braver. If you continually dive in and do the thing you're scared of, you'll experience what's known as progressive desensitization. In other words, the more you do something, the less you'll fear it. As you do the thing you fear more and more — whether it be public speaking, swimming out of your depth or removing spiders from your bathtub — you'll start to wonder what it was that you were so afraid of.

"Whatever you can do, or dream you can do, begin it. Boldness has genius, power, and magic in it!"

– GOETHE

"Never bend your head. Always hold it high. Look the world straight in the face."

– HELEN KELLER

"Confidence is courage at ease."

– DANIEL MAHER

KEEP TRACK OF YOUR ACCOMPLISHMENTS

When you need to cultivate courage it can be incredibly helpful to look back on past achievements. Designate a special place in which you record and store your proudest moments. This could be a scrapbook, a photo album or a notice board. Stick in/put up certificates, photos, letters, emails…whatever it is that serves as an instant reminder of what you have achieved. Looking through these things will boost your self-confidence and provide valuable motivation.

"Have the courage to make the change, the strength to see you through it, and faith that everything will turn out for the best."

– UNKNOWN

"He who is not courageous enough to take risks will accomplish nothing in life."

– MUHAMMAD ALI

GAIN PERSPECTIVE

When we get wrapped up in ourselves it is very easy to lose perspective. Take some time out to remind yourself what a tiny part of the universe you are. Look up into a clear night's sky and gaze at the stars, or meditate on images of vast landscapes. Reminding yourself of the size and scope of the universe does wonders for your perspective. So what if you forget a few of your words when speaking in public, or if you get turned down for promotion/a business loan/a date…? The world will still keep turning. Such thoughts may just give you the courage to try.

"There can be no failure to a man who has not lost his courage, his character, his self respect, or his self-confidence. He is still a King."

– ORISON SWETT MARDEN

DON'T HESITATE

Stop waiting until you're 100% ready to embark on your project or goal. This will never, ever happen. There will always be elements — emotional, financial, practical, hypothetical — that will hold you back. If you wait until your situation is perfect you will be waiting forever. Don't hesitate, just go for it!

"She took the leap and built her wings on the way down."

– KOBI YAMADA

"I have failed over and over and over again in life. That's why I succeed."

– MICHAEL JORDAN

LIGHTEN UP

If you take whatever you're about to do too seriously then the fear surrounding it builds up. If you can relax a bit, lighten up and realize that what you need to do is neither life threatening nor impossible you are far more likely to go ahead and do it. Acknowledge that most of what's making the prospect a scary one is the manner in which you are responding to it, not the thing itself.

"'It's impossible,' said pride.
'It's risky,' said experience.
'It's pointless,' said reason.
'Give it a try,' whispered
the heart."

– UNKNOWN

"She believed she could so she did."

– UNKNOWN

HARNESS YOUR POWER ANIMAL

While the concept of a power animal derives from shamanism, you don't have to be in any way religious or spiritual in order to access an animal guide; you simply need to use your imagination. Your power animal can be anything you want it to be, just let it become a symbol of your strength and resilience. Don't feel you have to conjure up an animal typically synonymous with courage and power — some very successful friends of mine, for example, harness Power Ducks in times of need. Whenever you need a bravery boost, simply visualize your power animal alongside you and together you can take on the world!

"The ultimate definition of bravery is not being afraid of who you are."

– CHOGYAM TRUNGPA

"Inaction breeds doubt and fear. Action breeds confidence and courage. If you want to conquer fear, do not sit at home and think about it. Go out and get busy."

– DALE CARNEGIE

INVITE POSITIVE FEEDBACK

When you have succeeded in something or accomplished a goal, tell people! We so often fall into the trap of only talking to friends about what worries us and what we're failing at. While this kind of support is vital, remember to also seek feedback from friends and family to reinforce the positive outcome of your actions. The more positive feedback you get from those around you, the more inspired and motivated you'll be to succeed again.

"Feel the fear and
do it anyway."

– SUSAN JEFFERS

"Trust yourself.
You know more
than you think
you do."

– BENJAMIN SPOCK

REALLY WANT IT!

Whatever it is you need to find the courage to achieve, make sure you really, really, really, really want it! Make a list of all the reasons why you want to accomplish your goal. This positive spin on your ambitions will naturally spur you into action — you won't have to force it if your desire is strong enough.

"May your choices reflect your hopes, not your fears."

– NELSON MANDELA

DEVELOP YOUR SELF-AWARENESS

If you can recognize the circumstances that make you doubt yourself, you can be proactive in removing yourself from those situations. Note down the scenarios that trigger self-doubt. Perhaps it's talking to a particular family member or colleague that always leaves you feeling negative and questioning your own decisions, or attending a certain meeting at work, engaging in particular activities…whatever it is that fuels your self-doubt and resistance to move forward, raise your self-awareness of it so next time you can act against and in spite of it.

"Owning our story and loving ourselves through that process is the bravest thing that we'll ever do."

– BRENÉ BROWN

FOLLOW YOUR INSTINCT

If you have a gut reaction to something, chances are it's a valid one as it comes from intuition as opposed to your ego. Trust your own intuition and move forward before deliberation fuels your self-doubt and fears.

"Go confidently in the direction of your dreams. Live the life you have imagined."

– HENRY DAVID THOREAU

"A bird sitting on a tree is never afraid of the branch breaking, because her trust is not on the branch but on its own wings. Always believe in yourself."

– UNKNOWN

"Whenever you find yourself doubting how far you can go, just remember how far you have come. Remember everything you have faced, all the battles you have won, and all the fears you have overcome."

– UNKNOWN

DON'T LOOK TO OTHERS FOR VALIDATION

You are the controller of your own destiny, and while it's important to seek support from loved ones, it should not be their validation that you wait on to push you forward. For success to have longevity, your motivation has to be intrinsic, i.e., come from within, so look inside yourself, not outwardly to others, to find the strength you need to pursue your goals and dreams.

"Everything you need, your courage, strength, passion and love; everything you need is already within you."

– UNKNOWN

"I was once afraid of people saying 'Who does she think she is?' Now I have the courage to stand and say, 'This is who I am.'"

– OPRAH WINFREY

FOCUS ON WHAT YOU CAN CONTROL

It's hard to act courageously when you're feeling out of control. Yet you will never have control over everything — you can control your actions, yet you have no control over the results of these. So focus on your actions and behavior, not the outcome.

"Courage doesn't always roar. Sometimes courage is the little voice at the end of the day that says I'll try again tomorrow."

– MARY ANNE RADMACHER

BE PRESENT

The simplest way to be present in the moment is to bring attention to your breathing for a few minutes. Grounding yourself in the present moment in this way puts you into a state of focused flow. You are more likely to stop overthinking your situation and to just get on with whatever work needs doing. If you remind yourself that all you can do is your best right NOW you will be able to put all of your energies into the task at hand.

"It's not who you are that holds you back, it's who you think you're not."

– UNKNOWN

"Confidence is the hinge on the door to success."

– MARY DUMAS

EVALUATE YOUR FEAR

Sometimes fear can be helpful — as humans we're wired toward self-preservation and the primal, instinctive response of fear can get us out of dangerous situations. However, in many day-to-day scenarios fear is far from helpful and if we respond to every fearful situation as if we're in mortal danger, i.e. we run a mile, we are unlikely to ever take risks and grow. So when you feel the fear, ask yourself if there is real threat, or if the threat is simply to your ego or sense of comfort.

"Don't worry about failures, worry about the chances you miss when you don't even try."

– JACK CANFIELD

"Storms make trees take deeper roots."

– DOLLY PARTON

TAKE A NEW PERSPECTIVE

We're often our own worst critics, much harsher on ourselves than we would be on others in the same situation. So take a step back and look at your scenario from a new perspective. Imagine you are listening to a good friend telling you about their goal. Would you focus on the pitfalls and "what ifs," or would you simply admire them for their strength and courage, pat them on the back and congratulate them for taking the risk?

"If you're brave enough to say goodbye, life will reward you with a new hello."

– PAULO COELHO

"Being deeply loved gives you strength; loving deeply gives you courage."

– LAO TZU

"The quickest way to acquire self-confidence is to do exactly what you are afraid to do."

– UNKNOWN

REHEARSE

We may well rehearse for a presentation or a speech, but why not try rehearsing for everything that makes you feel fearful? Being well prepared for a situation can really boost your bravery. So whatever is making you feel scared, practice it beforehand. Asking someone on a date, going for a job interview? Practice your lines out loud. Rehearse what you're going to say beforehand so you're less likely to be fumbling for words when the time comes to perform the task.

"You are never too old
to set another goal or
dream a new dream."

– C.S. LEWIS

"I quit being afraid when my first venture failed and the sky didn't fall down."

ALLEN H. NEUHARTH

SURROUND YOURSELF WITH BRAVE PEOPLE

Many studies have shown that behavior can be contagious. Our peer group can influence our thoughts, emotions and actions in innumerable ways. Surround yourself with people who make courageous decisions and some of that courage may just rub off on you.

"Courage is contagious. When a brave man takes a stand, the spines of others are often stiffened."

– BILLY GRAHAM

"You must become unshakable in the belief that you are worthy of a big life."

– KRISTIN LOHR

REMEMBER WE'RE ALL WINGING IT

If you're feeling too scared to take the first step toward a new direction in life, is it because you are comparing yourself to others who have made a similar move and are coming up short? That you're not as strong, intelligent, beautiful, deserving, confident, skilled or outgoing as them? Now is the time to remember that all of us — including the real grown-ups among us, the most powerful bosses — are winging it. Even the most successful, together-seeming people have their struggles. We're all just trying to find our way in an imperfect world.

"Don't let other people's opinions distort your reality. Be true to yourself. Be bold in pursuing your dreams. Be unapologetically you!"

– STEVE MARABOLI

LOVE YOURSELF

Practicing self-compassion is an incredibly important component in developing emotional resilience, essential in developing the courage required to live a full life. So be kind to yourself. Do not punish yourself for being a flawed, imperfect human being. Recognize when you are being overly self-critical and replace those harsh words with kind, loving ones.

"When you come to the end of your rope, tie a knot and hang on."

– FRANKLIN D. ROOSEVELT

"Never give up, for that is just the place and time that the tide will turn."

— HARRIET BEECHER STOWE

DON'T WORRY ABOUT OTHER PEOPLE'S OPINION OF YOU

Many of us spend too much time and energy worrying about what other people will think of us. What if we don't succeed in what we set out to achieve? What will people think? The truth is, very little. People are too busy in their own heads, consumed by their own thoughts, ideas, hopes, insecurities, dreams and failures to put yours under the microscope.

"What other people think of me is none of my business."

– DR. WAYNE W. DYER

"Whatever we expect with confidence becomes our own self-fulfilling prophecy."

– BRIAN TRACY

"Regardless of your lot in life, you can build something beautiful on it."

– ZIG ZIGLAR

WHAT'S THE WORST THAT COULD HAPPEN?

Self-doubt is fueled by disastrous predictions — often ones that have no grounding in reality. So ask yourself what's the worst that could happen. Consider the worst-case scenario and most likely you will realize that even if things go wrong, events are unlikely to be life altering. Keep things in perspective and don't let unfounded worries hold you back.

"Only those who will risk going too far can possibly find out how far one can go."

– T.S. ELIOT

"If you can imagine it, you can create it. If you can dream it, you can become it."

– WILLIAM ARTHUR WARD

"If you don't go after what you want, you'll never have it. If you don't ask, the answer is always no. If you don't step forward, you're always in the same place."

– NORA ROBERTS

STAND TALL

Adjusting your posture can have a big effect on how confident and motivated you're feeling. If you can project the air of confidence you will subsequently start to feel it. Try it for a day and see what a difference it makes; if you're sitting down, don't slouch but sit up straight with your shoulders back; walk with a determined stride and keep your head held high and your eyes on the horizon.

"The distance between your dreams and reality is called action."

– UNKNOWN

"There are those who look at things the way they are, and ask, why? I dream of things that never were, and ask, why not?"

– ROBERT KENNEDY

ASK QUESTIONS

If you are hesitant about a situation, get informed. Ask lots of questions or make sure you do your research. Remember that ignorance can contribute to worsening our fears. As we learn more about a situation, a person or an event then the fear surrounding them is likely to dissipate. Often it's the uncertainty that holds us back.

"Most of our obstacles would melt away if, instead of cowering before them, we should make up our minds to walk boldly through them."

– ORISON SWETT MARDEN

"Strength grows in the moments when you think you can't go on but you keep going anyway."

– UNKNOWN

TURN OBSTACLES INTO ASSETS

The most fearless people turn every obstacle they encounter into an opportunity. They are not daunted by challenges or put off course by disappointments and rejection. Try to see challenging events as gifts and utilize them to move forward. Rather than allowing them to stop you in your tracks let them motivate you to try harder.

"Do not speak badly of yourself, for the warrior that is inside you hears your words and is lessened by them. You are strong and you are brave. There is a nobility of spirit within you. Let it grow."

– DAVID GEMMELL

"If it's both terrifying and amazing then you should definitely pursue it."

– ERADA

ACCEPT PRAISE

A huge part of becoming a more confident and courageous person lies in accepting praise. When somebody praises you for something, don't discredit them as is so often our natural stock response. Instead, accept compliments with grace and openness. Let other people's positive assessment of you motivate you to succeed.

"With realization of one's own potential and self-confidence in one's ability, one can build a better world."

– DALAI LAMA

"Don't tell people your dreams, show them."

– UNKNOWN

LEARN TO SAY NO

Don't be fooled into thinking that to be open-minded, a courageous risk taker and to embrace a full life you need to say yes to everything and everyone all of the time. Learning how to say no will help you to stay focused and prevent you from taking wrong turns or getting involved with the wrong people.

"Courage is nothing more than taking one step more than you think you can."

– HOLLY LISLE

"Keep your fears to yourself but share your courage with others."

– ROBERT LOUIS STEVENSON

USE MUSIC

Music can have such a powerful effect on our mood, so why not use this to your advantage? If you need to pump yourself up for a big meeting, public speaking, a night out…listen to upbeat music. This mood booster, although temporary in itself, could be just the catalyst you need to trigger courageous action.

"Passion is what drives us crazy, what makes us do extraordinary things, to discover, to challenge ourselves. Passion is and should always be the heart of courage."

– MIDORI KOMATSU

"The thing about being brave is it doesn't come with the absence of fear and hurt. Bravery is the ability to look fear and hurt in the face and say move aside, you are in the way."

– MELISSA TUMINO

VISUALIZE YOURSELF BEING BRAVE

If you repeatedly visualize yourself successfully carrying out a fearful task with confidence, your subconscious mind will come to accept these visions as instructions for the task. Feed your mind with positive mental images of yourself acting with competence and courage and they may just become reality!

"To dare is to lose one's footing momentarily. To not dare is to lose oneself."

– SOREN KIERKEGAARD

"A hero is no braver than an ordinary man, but he is braver five minutes longer."

– RALPH WALDO EMERSON

EXERCISE

Regular exercise can dramatically alter your mindset, improve your energy levels and have a positive effect on mood. Get active and you will naturally feel more motivated, inspired and ready for action.

"We either make ourselves miserable or we make ourselves strong. The amount of work is the same."

– CARLOS CASTENADA

"There is no need to be ashamed
of tears, for tears bear witness that
a man has the greatest of courage,
the courage to suffer."

– VIKTOR FRANKL

"Out of your vulnerabilities will come your strength."

– SIGMUND FREUD

YOUR FUTURE SELF

Imagine a courageous future version of yourself. How would you start each day? What daily rituals would you have? Which bad habits would you have left behind? This will help you focus on what kind of person you need to become in order to stretch yourself and lead a full and courageous life.

"Being terrified but going ahead and doing what must be done — that's courage. The one who feels no fear is a fool, and the one who lets fear rule him is a coward."

– PIERS ANTHONY

"Sometimes life is about risking everything for a dream no one can see but you."

– UNKNOWN

VISUALIZE YOUR IDEAL LIFE

Your imagination is an incredibly powerful asset in creating your ideal life. Visualize yourself leading your dream life: Where are you? What are you doing? Who is alongside you? Focusing on exactly what it is you want is a great way to motivate yourself to go out and convert the dream into a reality.

"Every morning you have two choices: Continue to sleep with your dreams, or wake up and chase them."

– UNKNOWN

"All things are difficult before they are easy."

– THOMAS FULLER

BE AN OPTIMIST

While conventional wisdom suggests it's wise to expect the worst — that way you won't be disappointed when things go wrong and it'll be a pleasant surprise if things work out — much research has suggested that this isn't the most helpful attitude to adopt, that pessimism can undermine your performance creating a self-fulfilling prophecy.

"It takes a great deal of courage to see the world in all its tainted glory, and still to love it."

– OSCAR WILDE

"You may not always have a comfortable life and you will not always be able to solve all of the world's problems at once but don't ever underestimate the importance you can have because history has shown us that courage can be contagious and hope can take on a life of its own."

– MICHELLE OBAMA

DEVELOP A PLAN

Take a situation that you're fearful of and develop a plan. Create a tangible list to motivate you to overcome this fear. If, for example, the thing that's holding you back is fear of public speaking, your plan might include "practice your speech in front of one person you know well," building up to "perform your speech in front of a group of friends," and so on, increasing the fear factor in small increments. Getting a concrete plan down on paper may just be the catalyst you need to spur you into action.

"Focus on what you can do,
not what you can't. Small
steps turn into miles."

– UNKNOWN

"Pay attention to the things you are naturally drawn to. They are often connected to your path, passion, and purpose in life. Have the courage to follow them."

– RUBEN CHAVEZ

"Failure is not falling down but refusing to get up."

– CHINESE PROVERB

"The greatest oak was once a little nut who held his ground."

– UNKNOWN

BE CONFIDENT IN YOUR POTENTIAL

If you don't achieve a goal, tell yourself you will get closer next time. If someone criticizes you, instead of taking it to heart, take it as an opportunity to improve. If someone does better than you, learn from them. Take every setback as an opportunity for growth and have faith in your potential.

"Dare to be
remarkable."

– JANE GENTRY

"There is only one way
to avoid criticism:

do nothing

say nothing

and be nothing."

– ARISTOTLE

QUIT MOANING

Moaning about your lot in life, or about other people, is incredibly detrimental. This negativity will be a huge distraction from achieving your goals and forging out the life you want to live. So the next time you're about to moan about something or someone, take a deep breath and instead of voicing it, add something to your "to-do" list. Be positive and proactive.

"Courage doesn't mean we're not afraid anymore. It just means our actions aren't controlled by our doubts."

– BOB GOFF

"And then I realized that to be more alive I had to be less afraid so I did it. I lost my fear and gained my whole life."

– UNKNOWN

COPY COURAGEOUS BEHAVIOR

Emulate the actions of the bravest person you know, or someone in the public eye who inspires you. When you're lacking confidence, copying positive behavior can be a great way to start your own chain of confident, courageous actions.

"The Sun himself is weak when he first rises, and gathers strength and courage as the day gets on."

– CHARLES DICKENS,
THE OLD CURIOSITY SHOP

"F.E.A.R.
Has two meanings —
Forget Everything And Run
OR
Face Everything And Rise.
The choice is yours."

– UNKNOWN

DAILY STRENGTH

If you're stuck in a self-critical spiral, it can be helpful to remember just how strong and brave you are. You may not rappel from skyscrapers or jump out of planes on a daily basis, but maybe you are raising children, are a great friend or constantly helping people in small ways each day. Courage is not just about physical feats; more often it's about conquering the intangible fears that we encounter on a daily basis.

"Courage is only the
accumulation
of small steps."

– GEORGE KONRAD

"You didn't come
this far to only
come this far."

– UNKNOWN

EVALUATE YOUR EMOTIONS

If you are afraid to do something, ask yourself why. Challenge yourself by asking the following questions:

• What am I actually afraid of?

• How could this action harm me or anyone else?

• What could happen as a result of my action?

By evaluating your emotions in this way you are more likely to act rationally rather than based on an initial emotional response.

"She turned her can'ts into cans and her dreams into plans."

– UNKNOWN

DON'T WORRY

Accept that worrying is futile. Whatever situation you're facing, worrying won't help. Either do something about it or have the strength to let it go.

"Twenty years from now
You will be more disappointed
By the things you didn't do
Than by the ones you did.
So throw off the bowlines.
Sail away from the safe harbor.
Catch the trade winds in your sail.
Explore.
Dream.
Discover."

– MARK TWAIN

"Are you feeling a bit shaken, maybe stirred, maybe fearful and doubtful and completely, utterly, wildly terrified? Good. Keep going."

– VICTORIA ERIKSON

"Real courage…It's when you know you've been licked before you begin, but you begin anyway and see it through no matter what."

– HARPER LEE

"When you are living the best version of yourself, you inspire others to live the best versions of themselves."

– STEVE MARABOLI

PRACTICE GRATITUDE

Do not indulge in self-pity. Wallowing in thoughts of all that may not be right with your life will leave you demotivated and caught up in a spiral of negativity. Instead, focus on all that you have. Keep a gratitude journal and each night write down three things for which you are grateful. Focusing on all that you have, as opposed to what you are lacking, will encourage the positive mindset required to make healthy, courageous decisions.

"This could be your butterfly moment."

– TOPAZ

"Having courage does not mean that we are unafraid. Having courage and showing courage means we face our fears. We are able to say, 'I have fallen, but I will get up.'"

– MAYA ANGELOU

TRY REPEATING THESE MORNING MANTRAS TO EMBRACE AN ADVENTUROUS, OPEN SPIRIT AND QUELL ANY FEARS OF CHANGE:

- I love new experiences.

- I look forward to all of the adventures ahead of me.

- I am open and willing to live my life in new ways.

"The fishermen know that the sea is dangerous and the storm terrible, but they have never found these dangers sufficient reason for remaining ashore."

– VINCENT VAN GOGH

"Strength doesn't come from what you can do.

It comes from overcoming the things you once thought you couldn't."

– UNKNOWN

"Sometimes what you're most afraid of doing is the very thing that will set you free."

– UNKNOWN

VISUALIZE INACTION

Picture yourself a year from now as if you've done nothing to change your situation, made no moves toward accomplishing your goal. Regret can be a very powerful motivator.

"Courage is the power of
the mind to overcome fear."

– MARTIN LUTHER KING

"The bird who dares to fall
is the bird who learns to fly."

– UNKNOWN

REFRAME THE SITUATION

Framing is a behavioral technique used to shape how you think and feel about a situation. It's basically a way of relabeling whatever it is that is making you feel scared or anxious. If, for example, you're worried about an upcoming exam, reframe it as a "quiz," a job interview could become a "chat," a run can become a "jog." Reframing challenges to make them seem more commonplace can be a really effective way of mitigating the fear surrounding them.

"Life is either a daring adventure or nothing."

– HELEN KELLER

"Take risks. If you win, you will be happy. If you lose, you will be wise."

– UNKNOWN

PUT YOUR FEARS INTO WORDS

Write down a list of your fears. This can be difficult, it may make you feel embarrassed or ashamed, but persevere. Identifying and admitting your fears is the first step in facing them. Once you have completed your list, alongside each fear write down a plan of action as to how to overcome it.

"Always go with the choice that scares you the most, because that's the one that is going to help you grow."

– CAROLINE MYSS

"It's a terrible thing, I think, in life to wait until you're ready. I have this feeling that actually no one is ever ready to do anything. There is almost no such thing as ready. There is only now."

– HUGH LAURIE

"I remembered that the real world was wide, and that a varied field of hopes and fears, of sensations and excitements, awaited those who had courage to go forth into its expanse, to seek real knowledge of life amidst its perils."

– CHARLOTTE BRONTË, *JANE EYRE*

TREAD YOUR OWN PATH

Have the conviction to tread your own path through life, regardless of other people's expectations. Don't just follow a certain direction in life because that's the natural progression, and therefore what everyone will expect you to do. You don't have to take the path of least resistance, take the one less traveled if that one suits you better! Don't be afraid to do the unexpected.

"It is better to walk alone, than with a crowd going in the wrong direction."

– HERMAN SIU

"Her courage was her crown and she wore it like a queen."

– ATTICUS

GET HAPPY!

According to a Stanford Research Institute study a positive attitude contributes to success in life more than anything else. It suggests that 87.5 percent of people's success can be traced to their positive attitudes, while just 12.5 percent of their success comes from their aptitude, knowledge or skills. So try to focus on the positive — having fun in any situation can help you to build courage, distracting you from focusing on possible pitfalls.

"The first step to getting what you want is having the courage to get rid of what you don't."

– UNKNOWN

"The cave you fear to enter holds the treasure you seek."

– JOSEPH CAMPBELL

"In any given moment we have two options: To step forward into growth or to step back into safety."

– ABRAHAM MASLOW

BE ACCOUNTABLE

When setting out a plan to reach a specific target or make a particular change to your life, ask a friend to check up on your progress. Making yourself accountable in this way can be incredibly motivating.

"Be strong enough
to stand alone, smart
enough to know when
you need help, and brave
enough to ask for it."

– UNKNOWN

"You are not a drop in the ocean, you are the entire ocean in a drop."

– RUMI

MEDITATE

Fear-based thinking is often rooted in stress, so try managing your stress through meditation. If you're a beginner, look online for guided meditations tailored toward your specific requirements.

"One man scorned and covered with scars still strove with his last ounce of courage to reach the unreachable stars; and the world was better for this."

– MIGUEL DE CERVANTES,
DON QUIXOTE

"Courage, the original definition of courage, when it first came into the English language — it's from the Latin word cor, meaning heart — and the original definition was to tell the story of who you are with your whole heart."

– BRENÉ BROWN

DO WHAT MAKES YOU HAPPY

Countless studies have shown that happiness fuels success and performance, not the other way around. You need to create a life around what makes you happy in order to fulfill your potential.

"You have plenty of courage, I am sure," answered Oz. "All you need is confidence in yourself. There is no living thing that is not afraid when it faces danger. The true courage is in facing danger when you are afraid, and that kind of courage you have in plenty."

– L. FRANK BAUM,
THE WONDERFUL WIZARD OF OZ

"Dream as if you'll
live forever, live as if
you'll die today."

– JAMES DEAN

CHALLENGE YOUR THOUGHTS

Identify the negative beliefs you hold about yourself and find counter arguments to challenge these. Find evidence where you have acted in a way, displayed behavior or developed habits that contradict these negative ideas surrounding your sense of self. This will help you to realize that much of your sense of self-worth comes from unfounded perceptions rather than reality.

"If you hear a voice within you say 'you cannot paint,' then by all means paint, and that voice will be silenced."

– VINCENT VAN GOGH

"Trust yourself. Create the kind of self that you will be happy to live with all your life. Make the most of yourself by fanning the tiny, inner sparks of possibility into flames of achievement."

– GOLDA MEIR

DRESS FOR SUCCESS

When you look better, you feel better and so your self-esteem is automatically bolstered. So dress the part — choose your clothing to reflect the sort of person you want to be and where you want to be heading.

"If you're presenting yourself with confidence, you can pull off pretty much anything."

– KATY PERRY

"Trust the still, small voice that says, this might work and I'll try it."

– DIANE MARIECHILD

PRACTICE MAKES PERFECT

If your lack of confidence in a certain skill is holding you back, then practice it. Don't give in to the temptation to avoid situations where you have to use this skill, embrace them — the more you do it, the better at it you'll become and so your confidence and courage will grow.

"Don't get discouraged; it is often the last key in the bunch that opens the lock."

– UNKNOWN

"Courage is going from failure to failure without losing enthusiasm."

– SIR WINSTON CHURCHILL

LIVE YOUR LIFE BY EXAMPLE

Imagine becoming a role model for someone you care deeply about. Picture them copying your every move. Would you want them to remain unfulfilled and static in their life, or would you prefer they had the courage to go out and chase their dreams?

"Hope lies in dreams, in imagination, and in the courage of those who dare to make dreams into reality."

– JONAS SALK

"Each time we face our fear, we gain strength, courage, and confidence in the doing."

— THEODORE ROOSEVELT

SPEAK ASSERTIVELY

Adopt an assertive way of speaking — with confidence but without aggression. Look people in the eye when you address them and really engage. If you can get this way of communicating right you will ooze self-confidence and you will reach a place where others are far more likely to listen to you.

"You have brains in your head. You have feet in your shoes. You can steer yourself in any direction you choose. You're on your own. And you know what you know. You are the guy who'll decide where to go."

– DR. SEUSS

DEFINE YOUR VALUES

What really matters to you? What are your life values? Once you have defined these make a list of everything in your life that goes against them. Living contrary to your values is a fast track to negativity and feelings of low self-worth. So today identify one thing you could do to make your life step back in line with your values.

"Trust yourself.
You know more than
you think you do."

– DR. BENJAMIN SPOCK

WATCH YOUR INTERNAL DIALOGUE

Sometimes your inner voice can be your own worst critic, and an essential component of building self-confidence and therefore courage is to be kind to yourself. So next time your inner voice tells you "I'm a failure" or "I can't do this," simply switch it around. Say "I can do this!" Believe it, and you can.

"If you believe in yourself you can reach everything you want."

– KEES BROOS

"Live life as though nobody is watching, and express yourself as though everyone is listening."

– NELSON MANDELA

"It is not the mountain we conquer, but ourselves."

– SIR EDMUND HILLARY

THE WEEKLY CHALLENGE

Write down seven things you can do in the next seven days to move you toward your goal. Do this each and every week.

"If we all did the things we are capable of doing, we would literally astound ourselves."

– THOMAS ALVA EDISON

"If I have the belief that I can do it, I shall surely acquire the capacity to do it even if I may not have it at the beginning."

– MAHATMA GANDHI

"Successful people have fear, successful people have doubts, and successful people have worries. They just don't let these feelings stop them."

– T. HARV EKER

"Be who you are and say what you feel, because those who mind don't matter, and those who matter don't mind."

– BERNARD M. BARUCH

FIND ALLIES

Look for like-minded people who have similar passions and ambitions to your own. Discover forums and research associations and groups you could join, either for professional support, education or encouragement in your pursuits.

"My theory was that if I behaved like a confident, cheerful person, eventually I would buy it myself, and become that. I always had traces of strength somewhere inside me, it wasn't fake, it was just a way of summoning my courage to the fore and not letting any creeping self-doubt hinder my adventures. It's the process of having faith in the self you don't quite know you are yet. Believing that you will find the strength, the means somehow, and trusting in that, although your legs are like jelly. You can still walk on them and you will find the bones as you walk. Yes, that's it. The further I walk, the stronger I become."

– DAWN FRENCH

"But failure has to be an option in art and in exploration — because it's a leap of faith. And no important endeavor that required innovation was done without risk. You have to be willing to take those risks…"

– JAMES CAMERON

DEVELOP A "NEVER GIVE UP" ATTITUDE

One thing all successful and courageous people have in common is that they never give up. They persist through their fears, setbacks and self-doubt. Tell yourself that you can accomplish anything if you stick to it.

"You just can't beat the person who never gives up."

– BABE RUTH

"Champions keep playing until they get it right."

– BILLIE JEAN KING

MAKE ACTIVE CHOICES

Instead of leading a mediocre life by default, make active choices. Decide that from today onward you will not just drift into the middle-of the-road path, instead you will make active decisions that will forge the path you desire.

"The courage of life is often a less dramatic spectacle than the courage of a final moment, but it is no less than a magnificent mixture of triumph and tragedy.

People do what they must — in spite of personal consequences, in spite of obstacles and dangers and pressures — and that is the basis of all human morality."

– JOHN F. KENNEDY

"I'd rather regret the risks that didn't work out than the chances I didn't take at all."

– SIMONE BILES

SIMPLIFY

Cut the physical clutter from your life and you may just find your courage levels soaring. So many of us accumulate too much "stuff." We're then fearful of being unable to hold on to this material wealth if we take risks. Try to live a simpler life with fewer possessions.

PUT ON YOUR ROSE-TINTED SPECTACLES

There's a lot to be said for making believe everything's rosy. Spend some time in nature and notice the beauty in the world. Look for the best in everything and you'll soon start to see life as an adventure rather than a series of challenges.

"Begin doing what you want to do now. We are not living in eternity. We have only this moment, sparkling like a star in our hand-and melting like a snowflake."

– FRANCIS BACON

"It is confidence in our bodies, minds, and spirits that allows us to keep looking for new adventures."

– OPRAH WINFREY

TRUST IN YOUR UNIQUENESS

Believe that you have a gift to offer, one that nobody else on earth can. Nobody brings to the table exactly what you do. Trust in the fact that you are the best candidate for that job, the perfect partner for somebody or the ideal business proposition…

"You are the only person on earth who can use your ability."

– ZIG ZIGLAR

"You may be disappointed
if you fail, but you are
doomed if you don't try."

– BEVERLY SILLS

"Pride is holding your head up when everyone around you has theirs bowed. Courage is what makes you do it."

– BRYCE COURTENAY

"Walk amongst the natives by day,
but in your heart be Superman."

– GENE SIMMONS

LET GO OF EMBARRASSMENT

A fear of looking silly, inexperienced, weak or uneducated holds so many of us back. Today, let go of this fear of making a fool of yourself. Other people will have forgotten whatever foible you may or may not make long before you do.

"Mistakes are always forgivable, if one has the courage to admit them."

– BRUCE LEE

"Without courage,
wisdom bears no fruit."

– BALTASAR GRACIAN

CONSIDER YOUR IMPACT

Consider the impact of your courage on those around you. How will your loved ones benefit from you getting that new job, writing a novel or starting a business, for example? Make a list of everyone who would benefit and in what way. This could just be what motivates you to get started!

"The moment you doubt whether you can fly, you cease forever to be able to do it."

– J.M. BARRIE

"You can have anything you want if you are willing to give up the belief that you can't have it."

– DR. ROBERT ANTHONY

TAKE RESPONSIBILITY

You are where you are in life because of the decisions and actions (or inaction) you have taken. At each stage in life you have made choices that have brought you here. By acknowledging your responsibility in this way you are empowering yourself to shape the future — in whatever way you choose.

"How few there are who have courage enough to own their faults, or resolution enough to mend them."

– BENJAMIN FRANKLIN

"Fortune favors the brave."

– PUBLIUS TERENCE

"The courage to be is the courage to accept oneself, in spite of being unacceptable."

– PAUL TILLICH

"Don't waste your energy trying to change opinions…do your thing, and don't care if they like it."

— TINA FEY

TAKE TIME OUT

It may feel counterintuitive to just stop what you're doing when you're aiming high, but in order to maintain a motivated and courageous mindset, that is exactly what you need to do. If you are constantly exhausted and stressed it's pretty much impossible to be confident and courageous in the pursuit of your goals, so take time out for relaxation. Spend 30 minutes each day walking, reading a book, listening to music or chatting with friends… whatever it is that helps you to relax, and watch your motivation levels soar.

"Well done is better than well said."

- BENJAMIN FRANKLIN

FOCUS ON ONE THING AT A TIME

If you're now feeling inspired and brimming with courage, don't be tempted to take on everything in one go. If you decide — for example — that you want to run a marathon, leave a toxic relationship, change jobs, move to a new city, go back to college and lose weight, that's great. But you don't need to do it all at once. If you attempt to, you'll end up bouncing around in a crazed and non-productive fashion. Instead, narrow your focus and tackle one task at a time.

FORGIVE YOURSELF

Living in the past and dwelling on previous mistakes will only serve to hinder your progress. Today, make the decision to forgive yourself for all of your past failings. You will walk lighter and feel braver if you can do this.